Wall of Honor:
A Celebration of Fayetteville's Everyday Heroes

Dorothy Ellen Watkins Fielder

Dr. Marian Tally Simmons Brown

Photos and Design: Donna Fielder Barnes

Copyright 2019   by   Dorothy Ellen Watkins Fielder
Dr. Marian Tally Simmons Brown
Photographs and design: Donna Fielder Barnes

All rights reserved.

No part of this publication may be reproduced, stored in a retrieval system, or transmitted in any form or by any means, electronic, mechanical, photocopying, recording, or otherwise, without written permission of the publisher, except by a reviewer who may quote brief passages in a review.

For information regarding permission, write to:

Donna Barnes   122 Nelson Street, Durham, NC 27707   Wall.of.Honor.fay@gmail.com   919-368-5258

Categories :   1- Local African American history   2- Heroes   3- Black culture   4- Public Art

5- Young Adult literature   6- School and Community projects   7- Unity

Summary:

Wall of Honor is a show-and-tell book about the mural painted in the College Heights neighborhood in Fayetteville, North Carolina. The mural visualizes African American history through the eyes of folk in one neighborhood. It shares stories of everyday heroes and heroines who overcome adversities to build a strong community, based on faith and unity.

First printing 2019

ISBN   978-1-7337993-0-0   softcover edition

Dedication

Nancy Fortune Mebane Clark-Shakir: Activist

August 29, 1939 – February 5, 2017

Acknowledgments

Honoring Fayetteville's everyday heroes and heroines was a twenty-six year undertaking.

I appreciate the children, youth, adults and artists who suggested the persons to be painted or listed on the *Wall of Honor*.

Next, I thank residents who shared their personal historical knowledge: Charles "Ben" Evans (College Heights) and Joann Adams (Old Wilmington Road).

I appreciate the assistance and direction about the narrative by Donna Fielder Barnes, Dr. Marian Tally Simmons Brown, Darcy "Ghana" Fielder, Barbara Armstrong White, Tareva Johnson, Carole B. Weatherford, Wanda Wesley and Fred Whitted.

I thank Lallie Essie Scott Watkins, Geraldine "Jeri" Pratt, Jerome Johnson, Kirk de Viere, Umoja Group, Inc. members, and Nicholle Young (Archives Technician- Fayetteville State University) for their support and encouragement.

Lastly, thanks to Dorothy Ruff and the Loyal Senior Citizens' Club,
Dr. Annie McCullough Chavis plus Meta Weaver-Coaxum and the Fayetteville / Cumberland County Association of Black Social Workers (ABSW),
and Dr. Paula Quick Hall and the African American Education & Research Organization (AAERO), whose group discussions were helpful.

Original Artists 1994-2000
Dr. Francis Baird: Art Director
Ulysses Davis: Asst. Art Director

Roszella M. Williams

Fred Stanley Jr.

Rollinda Thomas

Ivy Wright

Susan Weaver

Patricia Capel

Reginald Foushee

Reginald Foushee II

Paul Lanier Jr.

Jason Thompson

James Thompson

Darryl Hall

Warren L. Moses Jr.

Wanda Wesley

Dorothy Finiello

Soni Martin: Coordinator —
FSU Art students

Artists 2001-2019
Ulysses Davis: Art Director
Mark Buku: Visiting Artist (Ghana)

Connie Monroe: Lead Artist

Roszella M. Williams: Lead Artist

Darcy 'Ghana' Fielder: Design Artist

Anthony Morrison

Melvin Tisdale

Jerome Johnson

Winson Clark

Sarah Lynn Brown

UChenna Aikens

George Alexander

Melvin Lindsay

Sandra Ross

Charlie Helms Jr.

Harvey Jenkins

Damien Mathis

Jalyn Bryant Standifer

Wanda Wesley

Gene Autry Brown

Susan Weaver

Franklin Arnold II, Lead Restore Artist

Dwight Smith: Coordinator —
FSU Art students

Helpers and Groups
Tiara Siner

Tetteh Effon

Dee Hardy

Zenzele Barnes

Yayra Tuprah

Kwami Tuprah

Marian T.S. Brown

Arianna Harmon

Kayla Johnson

Clarise West

Aaron Workeman

Terri Thomas

Jasmine Wright

Donna Barnes

Destiny Butts

David 'Dex' Fielder

Tyee Thomas

Jazzmyn Howard

Jaden Howard

Tony Woodard

T.J. Banks

Tina Hawkins

Zachariah Arnold

Adana Arnold

Zy'on Arnold

Daniel McMillan

E.E. Smith High School Art Class

Westarea Elementary School: 1994

Reid Ross Middle School: 1994

Luther 'Nick' Jeralds School: 1994

Fayetteville State Univ. Art Guild

Ulysses Davis

Dr. Francis Baird

CONTENTS

Dedication	1	Builders - Architects	17
Acknowledgements	2	Injustice Attacked	18
Artists	3	Spiritual People Praise Their Creator	19
Artists at Work	4	Mentors and Everyday Heroes	20
Introduction	6, 7	Military and Public Servants	21
Mural Coordinator	8	E.E. Smith High School	22
West African Culture: Adinkra Symbols & Proverbs	9	Sister Schools	23
West African Culture: Art	10, 11	Good Citizens and Role Models	24, 25
Africa, a poem by Carole Boston Weatherford	12	Unity and Teamwork	26
Voyage of Sorrow	13	Future Direction	27
Bound and Chained	14	References	28
Cash Crops	15	Writers	29-31
Tobacco	16		

Through artistic images, the *Wall of Honor* displays stories about an African American Neighborhood --- its people, struggles, values, traditions and culture.

The *Wall of Honor* stretches three-quarters of the first block of Langdon Street between Murchison Road and Slater Avenue, located in Fayetteville, North Carolina. It is directly across the street from Fayetteville State University's football field.

Although some Blacks came to America as explorers, free, or as indentured servants, most were kidnapped from West Africa and cast into slavery. Segregation was strictly followed in the South, but also practiced across America.

Hence, the journey for African Americans, since their arrival, has been a continual battle for freedom, justice, and equality. Fayetteville's Black residents fought to both survive and thrive. The College Heights neighborhood earned a reputation of producing many everyday heroes. The heroes on the Wall are ordinary people who tried to do right, attempted to live right and worked to bring right treatment for all. They struggled to make life better for themselves, their children and others in the community. The mural was painted to acknowledge and honor them, under the direction of Dr. Francis Baird (Fayetteville State University Art Instructor) and Ulysses Davis (Teacher / Community Artist). Eleven months, eighteen artists, and one hundred helpers later, the *Wall of Honor* was completed. Periodically, neighborhood residents touched up the images.

Mural Coordinator

School Social Worker Dorothy Fielder organized a group at E.E. Smith High School called Together Everyone Achieves More (TEAM Club). The twenty high-risk students' interests were not academic, nor musical, or athletic; they liked trips. The social worker found an ideal project: transform an unsightly, plain ugly, 160-foot long retaining wall into a historical and beautiful work of public art. During 1993 and 1994, TEAM Club members left Smith campus and took short trips to Langdon Street and painted a mural.

WEST AFRICAN CULTURE: Adinkra Symbols & Proverbs

Anthropologists consider Africa the birthplace of mankind. The cultural heritage of West Africa is vast and glorious; it includes art, sculpture, textiles, folktales, music and dance.

KENTE is called the 'talking cloth'. The vibrant colors, designs and patterns have meaning, and are worn on special occasions. This kente cloth honors Dr. Kwame Nkrumah's Egyptian wife – Fathia Fata. In 1957, Nkrumah became the first president of Ghana after British colonial rule.

The symbols, from top to bottom:

GYE NYAME:
God is Supreme:
Fear no man, Except God.

SANKOFA:
Reach back, gather
the best from the past
and move forward.

NKONSONSON:
Strength lies in unity:
Brotherhood and community.

WEST AFRICAN CULTURE: Art

The Senufo carver chose slit eyes and puckered mouth to indicate deep concentration, while horns denoted strength. The Benin artists used iron casts to form their masks of bronze, or carved them from ivory.

These three masks display the creativity, character, and complexity of African art. During colonial rule much of West African art was stolen and now can only be viewed in European and American museums.

'Coming of age' masks represent a time when traditions were taught, responsibilities learned, and secrets shared.

Africa
by Carole Boston Weatherford

Africa's not just some far-off place.
It's the beat of your heart and the sun in your face.

It's grand, old pyramids near the river Nile
and elders naming a newborn child.

It's coconuts dangling from tops of trees
and grasses dancing in the breeze.

It's herds of zebra striped black and white,
and mighty lions that stalk at night.

It's the elephant, giant of the land.
It's cloth and baskets made by hand.

It's monkeys swinging on jungle vines,
and riches deep in the darkest mines.

It's the thump, thump, thump of a talking drum.
It's where man's march first started from.

No, Africa's not so far away
for it is inside us to stay.

VOYAGE of SORROW

Slavery was the most disgraceful and horrific system practiced in American history. Beginning in 1500, the institution of slavery lasted three centuries. As many as 20 million Africans - either sold or stolen - endured separation from loved ones, then were subjected to brutality from strangers. Most enslaved Africans came from countries along the coast of West Africa. Fear was the captives' traveling partner, and pain their constant burden. The voyage across the Atlantic Ocean held the most miseries. Arrival on America's plantation solidified their status: slaves in bondage subject to inhumane treatment.

BOUND and CHAINED

The kidnapped Africans gaze straight ahead. Bewildered and disoriented, they summon up memories of home. They remember the earthy smells of palm fronds draped over the tops of their round huts. They hear the syncopated rhythm of water slapping the shore overgrown with scrub brush. In the compound they see Nana pound fufu and Baba mend fishing nets. Shivering sobs escape their cracked lips as they watch bare-bottom toddlers scamper about like grass cutters (squirrels) in the fields.

CASH CROPS

Tobacco and cotton grow in hot climates. Africans arrived with the knowledge of how to plant, tend and harvest these crops. For Southern plantation owners these crops had tremendous commercial value. As selling and trading spread north, west and overseas, Africans' free labor laid the foundation for America's riches and rank in the world.

TOBACCO

Captive Africans worked in the fields growing crops and in the homes cooking, cleaning and tending children. They cared for the livestock, drained swamps, dug canals, cleared woods, laid roads, and constructed homes, bridges and buildings. In essence, they did most of the work that bolstered the economy and increased America's wealth and world power.

BUILDERS – ARCHITECTS

Black men, free and enslaved, were involved in the building trades; they were carpenters and brick layers. John Patterson and Thomas Grimes, both freemen, were skilled builders. They played crucial roles in planning the construction of residences, commercial buildings and the Market House.

INJUSTICE ATTACKED

The haphazard mix of reds, purples and maroons suggest further dangers awaiting the captured. Terrorists hover above the Market House. Many who struggle die, so warriors must gather. Natural leaders, ordinary folk join groups that fight for freedom and justice. Positive institutions produce gains, yet the battle for full human rights is never won. FIGHT ON.

SPIRITUAL PEOPLE PRAISE THEIR CREATOR

Ministers in local churches preached messages of hope. Moses led his people out of slavery; the believers identified with this story. The tradition of spirituals and gospel songs reinforced positive themes that "trouble won't last always" and "better days is comin."

MENTORS and EVERYDAY HEROES

Fathers, church mothers, grandparents, teachers, coaches, scout leaders, nurses, and ministers were dedicated to service. They guided and inspired the next generation of youth who became distinguished medical doctors, lawyers, scientists, nationally recognized athletes, scholars, entrepreneurs, educators, and outstanding community leaders.

MILITARY and PUBLIC SERVANTS

Fayettevillians served in the United States military with honor from the Revolutionary War to the military conflicts of the 21st century. Levi and Mamie Evans, a College Heights family, had eight sons in all branches of the Military except the Coast Guard. Also from College Heights, U.S. Marine Joyce Malone was the first Black female to graduate from jump school and earn wings.

U.S Army Specialist/SFC Lawrence Joel served in the Korean and Vietnam Wars. He was awarded the Silver Star and the Medal of Honor for heroism.

Segregation was the way of life until the early 1970s. Therefore, African Americans developed thinking, analyzing, speaking, listening and leadership skills in churches, scouts, 4-H groups, schools, and Historically Black colleges. When opportunities opened they used these skills to become city councilmen, county commissioners, and elected officials of city and state agencies.

E.E. SMITH HIGH SCHOOL

"Born of Need, Destined to Serve, Striving to Excel" describes the mission of E.E. Smith High School. Unique among high schools, the proud Golden Bulls return from near and far for a National Alumni reunion each Memorial Day weekend. Cherished rituals are repeated: classmates gather to share memories, Smith 16 sings, Magnificent Marching Band struts, and graduating seniors are awarded scholarships.

SISTER SCHOOLS

College Heights children went to Newbold Training School, Orange Street School, Washington Drive Junior High, E.E. Smith High School and on to Fayetteville State Teachers College (now Fayetteville State University). Teachers impressed upon students that they were not limited by the social stigmas of the day. They were described as sister schools because teachers cared about students, and students cooperated with teachers. All, including the community's citizens, were committed to education.

In the 1950s small brick homes were built for teachers and staff who worked at Fayetteville State Teachers College. Home ownership was prevalent there, and in the surrounding areas. College Heights earned a reputation for being a strong and stable community.

GOOD CITIZENS and ROLE MODELS

UNITY and TEAMWORK

A call went out for Unity. Together everyone achieves more. Build a Neighborhood Watch that identifies problems and finds solutions. Share information with neighbors. Get involved in the community; VOLUNTEER. Know your rights and responsibilities. VOTE!

Hopefully, the neighborhood mural project is a public reminder for people who view it: you don't have to be a figure on the national stage to make a difference. Don't we all have an important role to play in our families, churches, organizations, and communities?

This pictorial book is the first in a series. It recognizes some everyday heroes and shares basic background historical information.

Writing the second book is already in progress. It includes specific stories about people depicted on the *Wall*. However, the *Wall* can never hold the portraits or names of all Fayetteville and Cumberland County citizens considered everyday heroes.

You can help.

We are calling on seniors, family members, neighbors, and amateur historians who remember people who fought to improve conditions in their communities. Do you know folks who nurtured children or adults? Do you know folk who stood up for their rights and the rights of others? Do you think these people should be recognized? If so, you have an important role to play in this community project.

Learn how.   See our website WallofHonorFay.wixsite.com/heroes for information.

FUTURE DIRECTION

REFERENCES

Barnes, Zenzele. *Wall of Honor: A Celebration of Fayetteville's Everyday Heroes.* ZKB Video Productions, Fayetteville, NC, 2018.

Nelson, Kadir. *Heart and Soul: The Story of America and African Americans.* New York: Harper Collins Publishers, 2011.

Weatherford, Carole Boston. Design by Jeffery Weatherford. *Africa.* Great Brain Entertainment, 2013.
Poem used by permission of the author. Pg. 12

Whitted, Fred. *Fayetteville, North Carolina: Black America Series.* Charleston, SC: Arcadia Publishing, 2000.

Photo credit: McEachan, David. *Gray Pyramid on Desert Under Blue Sky.* pexels.com Pg. 12

Dorothy Ellen Watkins Fielder

I was born and reared in Penn Township, a rural area outside of Pittsburgh, Pennsylvania. My family consisted of Mama, Poppa, seven brothers and one sister. After high school I was fortunate to attend Tuskegee Institute (now Tuskegee University) in Alabama, then I went on to earn a master's degree from Case Western Reserve University in Cleveland, Ohio. Presently, I am a retired widow, mother of five adult children, eight grandchildren, and twelve great-grandchildren.

Since 1982 I've worked in Fayetteville, North Carolina, as a children's protective service worker and a school social worker at E.E. Smith High School.

I enjoy developing programs that encourage, educate and inspire youth. I use strategies that highlight African American heritage, boost togetherness and unity, and increase participation of folk (young and old) in their community.

I believe the *Wall of Honor* project expanded interaction among neighbors and bolstered a more positive sense of community.

Dr. Marian Tally Simmons Brown

I am a Fayetteville native. I attended Newbold Training School, Orange Street School, and graduated from E.E. Smith High School. My parents were not professionals, but were working class; however, they got it in their heads to send their only child to the most prestigious private college for Black women: Bennett College, in Greensboro, North Carolina.

I took up the challenge and continued my education, receiving both M.M.E. and D.M.E. degrees from Indiana University, in Bloomington. During my graduate years at Indiana I began researching Black culture and the Black aesthetic. For twenty years I was Professor of Fine Arts at Florida State College, Jacksonville, Florida.

My parents had sacrificed so much for me; my love and loyalty drew me back to Fayetteville in 1992 to be their caretaker. My father was going blind and my mother developing Alzheimer's. From this difficult time I wrote the book: *"Grandma has Alzheimer's but it's O.K."*

After their deaths, I became more involved in the Fayetteville community. I received an 'Artists in the Schools' grant from the Arts Council to introduce a program that traced the history of African American music. I spoke on panels; organized seminars; and facilitated workshops about the Black Experience, Empowering Women through Arts & Culture, Memories of College Heights & E.E. Smith High, and Alzheimer's.

Donna Fielder Barnes

My parents met as college students at Tuskegee Institute (now Tuskegee University) in Alabama. They made a home in Syracuse, New York where they raised me, my three brothers and my sister. I grew up enjoying school, sports, music, summer camp and summer travels. I earned a bachelor's degree from Stanford University in Human Biology. I work as a Medical Laboratory Technologist at the University of North Carolina at Chapel Hill School of Dentistry.

I have been the family (and friend) photographer for many years and learned about layout from designing family photo books. Currently I live in Durham, North Carolina with my husband and daughter, and spend most of my free time line dancing.

www.ingramcontent.com/pod-product-compliance
Lightning Source LLC
Chambersburg PA
CBHW040301100526
44584CB00004BA/297